THE HUMAN BEHIND THE HERO
ANTHONY MACKIE
IS CAPTAIN AMERICA®

KRISTEN RAJCZAK NELSON

HOT TOPICS

Gareth Stevens
PUBLISHING

Please visit our website, www.garethstevens.com. For a free color catalog of all our high-quality books, call toll free 1-800-542-2595 or fax 1-877-542-2596.

Library of Congress Cataloging-in-Publication Data
Names: Rajczak Nelson, Kristen, author.
Title: Anthony Mackie is Captain America / Kristen Rajczak Nelson.
Description: Buffalo, New York : Gareth Stevens Publishing, [2023] | Series: The human behind the hero | Includes bibliographical references and index.
Identifiers: LCCN 2022018006 (print) | LCCN 2022018007 (ebook) | ISBN 9781538283714 (paperback) | ISBN 9781538283738 (library binding) | ISBN 9781538283745 (ebook)
Subjects: LCSH: Mackie, Anthony, 1978–Juvenile literature. | Motion picture actors and actresses–United States–Biography–Juvenile literature. | Captain America (Fictitious character)–Juvenile literature.
Classification: LCC PN2287.M175 R35 2023 (print) | LCC PN2287.M175 (ebook) | DDC 791.4302/8092 [B]–dc23/eng/20220524
LC record available at https://lccn.loc.gov/2022018006
LC ebook record available at https://lccn.loc.gov/2022018007

First Edition

Published in 2023 by
Gareth Stevens Publishing
2544 Clinton St
Buffalo, NY 14224

Copyright © 2023 Gareth Stevens Publishing

Designer: Rachel Rising
Editor: Kristen Nelson

Photo credits: Cover, p. 1 BAKOUNINE/Shuttterstock.com; pp. 1-32 KID_A/Shutterstock.com; pp. 1-32 gn8/Shutterstock.com; pp. 5, 29 Andrea Raffin/Shutterstock.com; p. 7 EQRoy/Shutterstock.com; pp.9,13 Everett Collection/Shutterstock.com; p. 11 PA Images / Alamy Stock Photo; p. 15 Storms Media Group / Alamy Stock Photo; p. 17 Tinseltown/Shutterstock.com; p. 19 Featureflash Photo Agency/Shutterstock.com; pp. 21, 25 PictureLux / The Hollywood Archive / Alamy Stock Photo; p. 23 Lifestyle pictures / Alamy Stock Photo; p. 27 lev radin/Shutterstock.com.

CPSIA compliance information: Batch #CW23GS: For further information contact Gareth Stevens, New York, New York at 1-800-542-2595.

Find us on

CONTENTS

BORN AND RAISED

Anthony Mackie was born on September 23, 1978, in New Orleans, Louisiana. He is the youngest of six brothers and sisters! He began acting in third grade. Later, he went to a school in New Orleans for kids learning about the arts.

BEHIND THE SCENES

ANTHONY WORKED IN CONSTRUCTION WITH HIS DAD WHEN HE WAS YOUNG. TODAY, HE STILL LOVES TO BUILD HOUSES!

FIRST STEPS

In 1997, Anthony started studying acting at the Juilliard School. The school is **prestigious** but at the time was known for having mostly white students. Anthony's class was one of the first to be very **diverse**. He moved to New York City to go there.

The Juilliard School

The Juilliard School
Irene Diamond Building

BEHIND THE SCENES

IN 2001, ANTHONY STARRED AS RAPPER TUPAC SHAKUR IN THE **OFF-BROADWAY PLAY** UP AGAINST THE WIND. PEOPLE STARTED NOTICING HIM!

ON THE BIG SCREEN

Anthony got even more attention in his first movie. He appeared with rapper Eminem in *8 Mile* in 2002. He has said the movie was a huge step right at the beginning of his **career**.

BEHIND THE SCENES

ANTHONY APPEARED IN WELL-KNOWN MOVIES SUCH AS *MILLION DOLLAR BABY* IN 2004 AND *HALF NELSON* IN 2006. *MILLION DOLLAR BABY* WON THE OSCAR FOR BEST PICTURE!

9

Anthony played Sergeant J. T. Sanborn in the movie *The Hurt Locker.* It was about the Iraq War and starred Jeremy Renner. **Critics** and fans thought Anthony was really good in it. The movie won the Oscar for Best Picture in 2010!

JEREMY RENNER

BEHIND THE SCENES

ANTHONY WASN'T **NOMINATED** FOR AN OSCAR FOR *THE HURT LOCKER*. HE WAS SO UPSET THAT HE TOOK A YEAR OFF FROM ACTING!

11

BECOMING A HERO

When Anthony was ready to work again, he emailed Marvel Studios. He wanted to be in a superhero movie! The first Marvel movie he tried out for was *Iron Man 3*. Instead, they brought him in to play Sam Wilson, who becomes Falcon.

MORGAN FREEMAN

BEHIND THE SCENES

ANTHONY IS FRIENDS WITH ACTOR MORGAN FREEMAN. MORGAN HAS GIVEN ANTHONY IMPORTANT CAREER ADVICE!

Anthony was excited to play Falcon. He said: "Growing up, I'd always loved Falcon, because he was a comic-book hero who was black who didn't have 'Black' in the title." He first appeared as Sam Wilson and Falcon in *Captain America: The Winter Soldier* in 2014.

DWAYNE JOHNSON

BEHIND THE SCENES

ANTHONY HAS TO BE IN GREAT SHAPE TO PLAY A SUPERHERO. HE FIRST GOT REALLY FIT FOR THE 2013 MOVIE *PAIN AND GAIN* AND WORKED OUT WITH DWAYNE JOHNSON AND MARK WAHLBERG!

JOINING THE AVENGERS

Anthony continued to play Falcon in more movies from Marvel Studios. He joined the Avengers in *Avengers: Age of Ultron* and was in *Ant-Man* in 2015. The next year he was in *Captain America: Civil War.* He was becoming a big star!

BEHIND THE SCENES

SINCE FALCON HAS NO SUPERPOWERS, ANTHONY SAYS: "I'M BASICALLY THE EYES AND EARS OF THE AUDIENCE, IF YOU WERE PUT IN THAT POSITION WHERE YOU COULD GO OUT AND FIGHT ALONGSIDE SUPERHEROES."

17

In 2018, Anthony again joined up with the Avengers for *Avengers: Infinity War*. The movie would go on to make more than $2 billion! The following year, *Avengers: Endgame* came out—and Anthony's next superhero journey began.

BEHIND THE SCENES

ANTHONY HAS FOUR SONS. HE TOOK HIS OLDEST SON TO THE PREMIERE, OR FIRST SHOWING, OF *ENDGAME*!

19

THE SHIELD

At the end of *Avengers: Endgame*, Steve Rogers, the character who had been Captain America up until then, gives his shield to Sam Wilson. Fans were stunned! Did that mean Anthony was going to be the next Captain America?

CHRIS EVANS

BEHIND THE SCENES

CHRIS EVANS, WHO PLAYED STEVE ROGERS AND CAPTAIN AMERICA IN *ENDGAME*, WAS THE ONE TO TELL ANTHONY ABOUT SAM RECEIVING THE SHIELD. THE TWO ARE GOOD FRIENDS!

When the TV show *The Falcon and the Winter Soldier* came out in 2021, Anthony was still playing Sam Wilson as Falcon. The character thought a lot about how people would feel about Captain America being a Black man. Anthony wondered about that too.

BEHIND THE SCENES

IN MARVEL COMICS, SAM WILSON BECAME CAPTAIN AMERICA IN AN ISSUE OF *CAPTAIN AMERICA* THAT CAME OUT IN 2014.

THE SUIT

Near the end of *The Falcon and the Winter Soldier*, Anthony finally became Captain America! The first time he put on the Captain America suit, he said, "I was excited, but openly **emotional**." The suit even had wings like Falcon's did!

BEHIND THE SCENES

THE FIRST CAPTAIN AMERICA WHO WAS BLACK WAS THE COMIC-BOOK CHARACTER ISAIAH BRADLEY, WHO FIRST WORE CAPTAIN AMERICA'S SUIT AND SHIELD DURING WORLD WAR II

REPRESENT!

Anthony knows how powerful it is for a Black kid to see a Black actor play such an **iconic** part. But he's said, "It's just as important for a Latino kid or a white kid or an Asian kid to see a Black Captain America."

BEHIND THE SCENES

ANTHONY IS PROUD TO PLAY CAPTAIN AMERICA AS A BLACK MAN: "IT SHOWS THE PROGRESS OF THE PEOPLE IN THIS COUNTRY, AND THE WAY WE THINK."

Anthony worked hard building his career. From a kid in New Orleans to a movie Avenger, he's come a long way. Now, he's set to star in the fourth Captain America movie. What else will he do?

BEHIND THE SCENES

ANTHONY WORKS TO PUSH FOR MORE REPRESENTATION IN ALL PARTS OF MARVEL MOVIES, IN FRONT OF THE CAMERA AND BEHIND IT.

TIMELINE

1978 ANTHONY MACKIE IS BORN ON SEPTEMBER 23.

1997 HE STARTS AT THE JUILLIARD SCHOOL.

2001 HE PLAYS TUPAC SHAKUR OFF-BROADWAY.

2002 HE APPEARS IN *8 MILE*.

2008 HE APPEARS IN *THE HURT LOCKER*.

2014 ANTHONY PLAYS SAM WILSON/FALCON IN *CAPTAIN AMERICA: THE WINTER SOLDIER*.

2015 *AVENGERS: AGE OF ULTRON* AND *ANT-MAN* COME OUT.

2016 ANTHONY APPEARS IN *CAPTAIN AMERICA: CIVIL WAR*.

2018 *AVENGERS: INFINITY WAR* COMES OUT.

2019 *AVENGERS: ENDGAME* COMES OUT. THE CAPTAIN AMERICA SHIELD IS PASSED TO ANTHONY AS SAM WILSON.

2021 *THE FALCON AND THE WINTER SOLDIER* COMES OUT. ANTHONY IS SHOWN IN A CAPTAIN AMERICA SUIT FOR THE FIRST TIME.

FOR MORE INFORMATION

BOOKS

Cowsill, Alan, and John Tomlinson. *Marvel Avengers: The Ultimate Character Guide*. New York, NY: DK Publishing, 2021.

Remender, Rick, et al. *Captain America: Sam Wilson - The Complete Collection Vol. 1*. New York, NY: Marvel, 2020.

WEBSITES

Anthony Mackie - IMDb
www.imdb.com/name/nm1107001/
Find out more about what Anthony Mackie has been up to on the big screen here.

Captain America (Sam Wilson)
www.marvel.com/characters/sam-wilson
Check out the official Marvel website about Sam Wilson's Captain America.

GLOSSARY

career: The job someone chooses to do for a long time.

critic: A person who writes or tells what they think about books, movies, and other art.

diverse: Made up of people who are different from each other.

emotional: Showing feelings, such as by crying.

iconic: Something that is well known by many.

off-Broadway: Having to do with theater shows in New York City that are smaller than most Broadway shows.

nominate: To suggest someone for an honor.

Oscar: One of many awards given yearly to the best movies, actors, and others who work in making movies.

prestigious: Having importance and honor.

representation: The inclusion of people of all ages, genders, and ethnicities in TV shows and movies as well as the workplace.

INDEX